Profiles of the Presidents

CALVIN COOLIDGE

★ ★ ★

...of the Presidents

CALVIN COOLIDGE

by Robin Doak

Content Advisers: William Jenney, Site Administrator, President Calvin Coolidge State Historic Site,
Plymouth Notch, Vermont; and Jim Cooke, historian, author, and actor, Quincy, Massachusetts
Reading Adviser: Dr. Linda D. Labbo, Department of Education, The University of Georgia

COMPASS POINT BOOKS ✦ MINNEAPOLIS, MINNESOTA

Compass Point Books
3109 West 50th Street, #115
Minneapolis, MN 55410

Visit Compass Point Books on the Internet at *www.compasspointbooks.com*
or e-mail your request to *custserv@compasspointbooks.com*

Photographs ©: White House Collection, Courtesy White House Historical Association (8), cover, 3;
Hulton/Archive by Getty Images, 7, 15, 19, 21, 28, 36, 41, 44, 47, 55 (right), 56 (right, all), 57 (top
left & right), 58 (top right); North Wind Picture Archives, 8, 54 (top); Mark E. Gibson/The Image
Finders, 9; Courtesy Vermont Historical Society, 10, 11 (bottom), 14, 54 (bottom); Calvin Coolidge
Presidential Library & Museum, 11 (top), 17, 56 (bottom left); Courtesy of the Black River Academy
and Historical Society, 12; Library of Congress, 13, 16, 23, 25, 29, 30, 31, 34, 35, 37, 38, 39, 55
(left), 56 (top left), 57 (bottom left); Bettmann/Corbis, 20, 26, 27, 32, 45, 46, 49, 58 (left);
Minnesota Historical Society, 24; Corbis, 42, 43; Lee Snider/Corbis, 50, 59 (left); E.O.
Hoppé/Corbis, 58 (bottom right); Stock Montage, 59 (right).

Editors: E. Russell Primm, Emily J. Dolbear, Melissa McDaniel, and Catherine Neitge
Photo Researcher: Svetlana Zhurkina
Photo Selector: Linda S. Koutris
Designer/Page Production: The Design Lab/Les Tranby
Cartographer: XNR Productions, Inc.

Library of Congress Cataloging-in-Publication Data
Doak, Robin S. (Robin Santos), 1963–
    Calvin Coolidge / by Robin Doak.
        p. cm. — (Profiles of the presidents)
Summary: A biography of the thirtieth president of the United States, discussing his personal life,
education, and political career.
Includes bibliographical references and index.
    ISBN 0-7565-0276-4 (hardcover : alk. paper)
    1. Coolidge, Calvin, 1872–1933—Juvenile literature. 2. Presidents—United States—Biography—
Juvenile literature. [1. Coolidge, Calvin, 1872–1933. 2. Presidents.] I. Title. II. Series.
    E792 .D63 2003
    973.91'5'092—dc21   2002153301

Table of Contents

★ ★ ★

★

NOTE: In this book, words that are defined in the glossary are in **bold** *the first time they appear in the text.*

The President from Vermont

★   ★   ★

As a child in Vermont, Calvin Coolidge learned the value of tradition, discipline, and hard work. Later, he drew on these lessons to become a successful politician.

Coolidge also had the good luck to be president during one of the most peaceful and wealthy periods in U.S. history. As the nation's leader, he believed that his job was to keep the country's economy healthy. He thought the best way to do this was to leave things alone and not try anything new or risky. During Coolidge's years as president, he cut taxes and kept the government out of private business. He was against giving aid to workers or other groups because he didn't think the U.S. **Constitution** allowed it. Coolidge's approach to government could best be summed up by one of his famous statements: "Four-fifths of all our troubles in this life would disappear if we would only sit down and keep still."

Today, Coolidge is best remembered for his personality. Nicknamed Silent Cal, he spoke only when he had something to say. Even then, he spoke in the shortest, most direct way possible. Coolidge once said, "If you don't say anything, you can't be called upon to repeat it."

◀ *Calvin Coolidge, the thirtieth president of the United States*

Growing Up in Plymouth Notch

★ ★ ★

Coolidge's birthplace ▸
is located in the
Plymouth Notch
Historic District
in Vermont.

John Calvin Coolidge was born on July 4, 1872, in Plymouth Notch, Vermont. He was named after his father, John Calvin Coolidge, but everyone called him Calvin.

◂ *A modern view of the Plymouth Notch general store, where John Coolidge worked*

The locals called their tiny village the Notch. The village center had seven houses, a church, a general store, and a few small shops. A number of other homes and farms lined the roads near the village center. Calvin's father ran the region's post office and general store for a time. The post office was in one corner of the general store, which was attached to the family's small, five-room cottage. The Coolidge's store was the center of the little town. It was an exciting place for a boy to grow up.

Calvin's mother was Victoria Josephine Moor. She died when Calvin was twelve years old. He never got over it. Years later, Coolidge wrote about his mother's death: "The greatest grief that can come to a boy came to me. Life was never to seem the same again."

John Coolidge had two small children to raise alone. Over the years, Calvin and his younger sister,

Victoria Moor ▶

Abigail, looked to their father for love and guidance. Calvin's father taught them to value hard work, common sense, honesty, and community service. As Calvin grew up, he also adopted his father's political beliefs. As an adult, he would join the Republican Party, the same party his father belonged to.

▲ *Calvin's younger sister, Abigail*

Calvin was a thin boy with red hair and freckles. He attended the one-room schoolhouse that served all the children in the area. After school, he helped out on the farm his father had bought when Calvin was four. By the time Calvin was twelve, he could plow with a team of oxen. He chopped wood, repaired fences, and helped harvest hay and corn. In the spring, he drew the sap from maple trees. He became an expert at boiling the sap down into maple sugar.

▲ *Calvin as a young boy*

Calvin (back row, ▲
second from left)
with his graduating
class at Black River
Academy in 1890

There was time for fun in Calvin's life, too. Years later, he recalled having plenty of time for "playing and wasting." He also remembered attending country fairs, the circus, picnics, and parties for young people.

When Calvin was fifteen, his father sent him away to school in Ludlow, a town not far from the Notch. Calvin attended the Black River Academy for three years. There he was introduced to the subjects of government, politics, and the U.S. Constitution. Calvin's interest in the Constitution would endure throughout his life.

Shortly before he graduated from high school in 1890, tragedy again struck the Coolidge family. Fifteen-year-old Abigail, who also attended Black River Academy, became ill and died. Calvin and his sister had been very close, and he missed her greatly. He wrote home to his father, "It is lonesome here without Abbie."

In 1891, Calvin entered Amherst College in Amherst, Massachusetts. Coolidge took his education at Amherst seriously. He studied hard, but at first his

▼ *Amherst College in the 1890s*

grades were only fair. He was homesick. He thought about leaving college, but his father encouraged him to stay. Coolidge did stay and was earning excellent grades by his last two years at Amherst. An essay he wrote in his final year of college titled "The Principles Fought For in the American Revolution," won a national prize of a gold medal worth $150.

Coolidge as a young lawyer ▼

Coolidge graduated from Amherst with honors in 1895. He was chosen by his classmates to give a funny speech on graduation day. Coolidge would always look back on his college years fondly. Later, as president, he would appoint some of his college friends to government jobs.

Law, Love, and Politics

★ ★ ★

After finishing college, Coolidge decided to study law. He spent the next two years working at a law office in Northampton, Massachusetts. There he learned every-thing he needed to know to become a lawyer. In 1897, Coolidge passed his law exams. He was then allowed to practice law in Massachusetts.

Coolidge quick-ly set up his own law practice and became involved in North-ampton politics. In

▼ Coolidge's home in Northampton, Massachusetts

1898, he ran for a seat as city councilman. Coolidge relied on his direct manner to win the seat. He went door to door telling voters, "I want your vote. I need it. I shall appreciate it." Coolidge won the election.

While practicing law and beginning his political career, Coolidge met Grace Anna Goodhue. She was a young teacher at the Clarke School for the Deaf in Northampton. Grace had graduated from the University of Vermont in 1902. Energetic, educated, fun-loving, and beautiful, Grace was the perfect balance for the quiet, serious Coolidge. The two Vermonters fell in love and were married in October 1905. The couple did not like to spend a lot of money, so they rented half of a two-family home in Northampton. They soon had two sons, John and Calvin.

Grace Coolidge ▼ in 1924

Through plenty of hard work, Coolidge slowly became involved in Massachusetts politics. In 1906, he won a seat in the state house of representatives. He served two terms there. As a state representative, he favored giving women the right to vote. He also favored having U.S. senators be elected directly by the people rather than by the vote of state **legislatures.** These measures never passed while Coolidge was a state representative, but he had the satisfaction of seeing them become law during his lifetime.

▼ *Coolidge as mayor of Northampton*

In 1909, Coolidge was elected mayor of Northampton. While mayor, he was able to reduce taxes and increase wages for teachers. In 1911, he was elected to the state senate, and he soon became the senate president. Then in 1915, he was elected lieutenant governor, the second highest office in the state.

Though his career had taken off, Coolidge was still **thrifty.** When the legislature was in session, he always stayed at the Adams House, a hotel on Washington Street in downtown Boston. He rented a single room for a dollar a day. On weekends, he took the train home to Northampton, where Grace was raising the boys. When Coolidge was elected lieutenant governor, he rented an additional room across the hall so that his family could visit him.

In 1918, Coolidge ran for governor of Massachusetts. During the **campaign,** he continued to use his direct manner to reach citizens. When he spoke to the public, he stuck to the issues of the day and stood firm to his ideals of honesty and plain speech. "I am responsible for what I have said and what I have done," Coolidge stated. "I am not responsible for what my opponents say I have said or say I have done . . . in untrue political advertisements and untrue posters."

Coolidge's straightforward manner appealed to many voters, and he won the election. World War I (1914–1918) had just ended, however, and the state was trying to adjust to peacetime. Coolidge supported giving workers more money, but he also opposed passing laws that would force businesses to do this. He even wrote the mayor of Boston urging that teachers be paid higher salaries.

Coolidge's term as governor probably would have gone unnoticed nationally if it hadn't been for one event in the fall of 1919. That autumn, Coolidge faced a serious crisis— the Boston police went on **strike.** In September, more than 1,100 of Boston's police officers walked off their jobs to protest low salaries, long hours, and dangerous working conditions. They wanted to join a **union** called the American Federation of Labor.

▲ *Governor Coolidge (front) with (from left) his son, John, his father, his son, Calvin Jr., and his wife, Grace*

Without the police to keep order, gangs of criminals roamed the city's streets. They broke into stores, damaged buildings, and attacked people unfortunate enough to cross their paths.

One of the few ▶ Boston policemen (left) still on duty in September 1919 speaking to a U.S. soldier

The mayor of Boston asked Governor Coolidge for help. Coolidge responded by sending in the state's **militia.** The militia broke up the strike and restored peace to the city. Samuel Gompers, the president of the American Federation of Labor, asked Coolidge to rehire the striking policemen and fire the police commissioner, Edwin U. Curtis. Coolidge refused. He sent a message to Gompers that read, "There is no right to strike against the public safety by anybody, anywhere, any time." This statement earned him fame across the country. Even Democratic president Woodrow Wilson praised Coolidge.

▼ Governor Coolidge inspecting members of the Massachusetts militia that were sent to break up the Boston police strike and restore order to that city in 1919

Road to the White House

★   ★   ★

Later that fall, Coolidge was reelected governor. His calm and successful handling of the Boston police strike had gained him important supporters in the national Republican Party. At the 1920 Republican convention, some people supported Coolidge for president. However, Senator Henry Cabot Lodge of Massachusetts said, "No man who lives in a two-family house is going to be president!" Coolidge was not able to gather enough support to become the Republican **candidate.** Instead, Senator Warren G. Harding of Ohio was chosen

The Republicans still needed to select a vice presidential candidate to run with Harding. Party leaders suggested Senator Irvine Lenroot of Wisconsin, but a man from Oregon stood on a chair and shouted "Coolidge!" Delegates eagerly agreed. Coolidge became Harding's running mate.

Harding and Coolidge could not have been more different. Unlike Silent Cal, Harding was easygoing, energetic, and talkative. During the campaign, both men kept low profiles. Harding remained close to his home in Marion, Ohio, and ran a "front-porch campaign."

▲ *The 1920 Republican National Convention took place in Chicago.*

Coolidge went on a speaking tour and visited a dozen southern states. Together, the two easily defeated the Democrats in the 1920 presidential election. This was the first U.S. election in which women were able to vote.

Warren G. Harding ▶
(third from left)
campaigning from a
train in Minnesota
in 1920

◄ *Coolidge (right) listened as President Harding spoke to members of the U.S. House of Representatives.*

As vice president, Coolidge gave a few speeches and attended meetings with the president and other top government officials. During these meetings, Coolidge was usually quiet.

During the summer of 1923, the vice president and his family went on a vacation to Plymouth Notch. On August 2, Coolidge's father woke him in the middle of the night with serious news: President Harding had died of a heart attack. The old Coolidge home had no electricity or telephone, so Coolidge went to a nearby general store to telephone government officials and make sure the news was true. Then, by the light of an oil lamp, he was sworn in as the thirtieth president of the United States by his father, a justice of the peace. After that, the new president went back to bed.

Coolidge suddenly held the nation's highest office. After returning to Washington, D.C., he was sworn in a second

In this interesting ▶ photo, Coolidge (left) and his father look like they are re-enacting the swearing-in ceremony that took place at the family home in Vermont. Actually, the photo shows Coolidge being sworn in as governor of Massachusetts. Coolidge's father posed for a picture showing where he stood at the time of the presidential swearing in. Then that photo replaced the Massachusetts official who was in the original photo. This historical photo is a fake!

time. Later, the new president penned a letter to a friend: "I am going to try to do what seems best for the country," he wrote, "and get what satisfaction I can out of it."

Coolidge had the opportunity to help his nation almost immediately after taking office. In the months before Harding's death, news of **corruption** and illegal acts by some of Harding's closest friends and advisers was revealed. Their actions included **bribery** and stealing millions of dollars of public money. The worst scandal of Harding's presidency broke after his death. His secretary of the interior had leased public oil reserves to private companies in exchange for large bribes. This was known as the Teapot Dome Scandal because the oil fields were located at Teapot Dome, Wyoming.

▾ *The U.S. Capitol becomes a teapot in this political illustration about the Teapot Dome Scandal.*

Former secretary of ▸ the interior Albert B. Fall (left), shown with oil executive Edward Doheny and their lawyers, was the first cabinet secretary ever sent to prison.

Coolidge handled the crisis quickly and effectively. Several officials involved in the corruption went to jail. The new president also demanded that others who had been involved in the scandal quit. Coolidge's honest, upright manner and plain speeches restored honor to the presidency. By simply being himself, he was able to gain the trust and respect of the American people.

After dealing with Harding's scandals, Coolidge settled into his new role as president. He established a daily routine, which he almost always followed. Every day, he rose early and ate breakfast. Then he worked until noon. At noon, he ate lunch. He next went for a walk and took a nap that might last as long as three hours. After his nap, the president returned to business for a while before attending a dinner or public event. On Tuesdays and Thursdays, Coolidge met with reporters. He held such **press conferences** more often than any other president.

As the nation's new president, Coolidge's chief goal was to keep the country's economy on track. To achieve this, he thought it was best to leave well enough alone. He believed that with time, most problems would straighten themselves out. Coolidge also thought that the government should stay out of private businesses and the U.S. economy as much as possible. This attitude is known as **laissez-faire** politics. *Laissez-faire* is a French phrase that means "let it be."

◀ *President and Mrs. Coolidge attending a garden party for World War I veterans at the White House. Public events like this one were part of Coolidge's daily routine.*

Silent Cal

★ ★ ★

Alice Roosevelt
Longworth with her
husband, Nicholas,
at an event in
Washington,
D.C., in 1926

After the scandals of Harding's term, Americans were ready for a president like Calvin Coolidge. He was very different from the man who came before him. Coolidge was quiet and solemn. He had an air of dignity that inspired trust, respect, and confidence. Not everyone who met him was impressed by his seriousness, however. Alice Roosevelt, the daughter of former president Theodore Roosevelt, said that Coolidge looked like he'd been "weaned on a pickle."

Coolidge was famous as a man of few words, and he encouraged people to think of him this way. Once at a dinner party, a woman sitting next to him said she had bet a friend that she could get Coolidge to say more than two words. Coolidge replied, "You lose."

Despite being a quiet man, President Coolidge delivered more public speeches than earlier presidents. Because of the radio, Americans across the nation were also able to hear presidential speeches delivered from Washington.

President Coolidge rarely dined alone. He held more parties and dinners

Coolidge delivering his first message to Congress in 1923

than any previous U.S. president. During these social events, Coolidge received help from his wife, Grace, who was charming and talkative with all the guests. As first lady, Grace Coolidge was beloved across the nation.

Grace Coolidge, ▶ shown standing on the lawn of the White House with her husband, was a gracious and charming first lady.

While the president was often seen as sour and silent, his wife was considered to be just the opposite. White House staff members called her Sunshine, a nickname that reflected her friendly, outgoing personality. Members of the press also loved her. They photographed her at every public appearance she made. Coolidge knew how helpful his wife was. "She is wonderfully popular," Coolidge wrote to his father. "I don't know what I would do without her."

Though the president often relied on his wife, he also made her follow many strict rules. He didn't allow Grace to fly in a plane, drive a car, or ride a horse. Nor would he permit his wife to wear pants, cut her hair short, or dance in public. At that time, many men expected their wives to follow rules like these.

Coolidge's most important rule was for Grace to remain silent on all political issues. She was not allowed to give interviews, and she could never be quoted by reporters. Instead, Grace kept busy with social causes. She visited hospitals and Girl Scout troops, winning admirers for herself and the president. One of her favorite causes was helping Americans with hearing problems. She raised funds, visited schools for the deaf, and hosted deaf students at the White House. She tried hard to raise awareness of the struggles faced by deaf people.

During her husband's presidency, Grace also met and became a close friend of Helen Keller, a deaf and blind woman who was a famous author and speaker.

Helen Keller (right) ▶ reading Grace Coolidge's lips with her hands

Coolidge, although a hard worker, loved nothing better than relaxing with Grace and his two sons. One of his first acts as president was to place a rocking chair on the front porch of the White House. He was content to sit and smoke the cigars that he loved so well. In 1923, Coolidge started a presidential tradition that continues to this day when he lit the first White House Christmas tree.

◄ Coolidge (right) began the tradition of lighting the White House Christmas tree on December 24, 1923.

Charles G. Dawes ▸

In 1924, one year after Harding's death, Coolidge ran for a full term as president. Illinois banker and politician Charles G. Dawes became his vice presidential running mate. Coolidge and Dawes ran a campaign based on "Coolidge **prosperity**." During the campaign, the president spoke about the nation's economic health. He promised to keep the country going in the same positive direction.

Unfortunately, tragedy struck during the campaign. The president's sixteen-year-old son, Calvin, had developed a blister on his foot while playing lawn tennis at the White House. The blister caused blood poisoning, and Calvin died in a Washington hospital.

◄ *The Coolidges at their son's grave in Northampton, Massachusetts, in 1928*

Young Calvin's death affected the president deeply. He delivered no more political speeches during the course of the campaign. Though Coolidge easily defeated the Democratic candidate John W. Davis and the Progressive candidate Robert M. La Follette, the mood inside the White House was somber. Coolidge later wrote, "In [Calvin's] suffering he was asking me to make him well. I could not. When he went the power and the glory of the Presidency went with him. . . . I do not know why such a price was exacted for occupying the White House."

President and Mrs. ▶ Coolidge and Senator Charles Curtis on their way to the Capitol for the 1925 presidential inauguration

The Roaring Twenties

★   ★   ★

Calvin Coolidge had now been officially elected president in his own right. In his speech after being sworn into office, Coolidge vowed to keep America's economy healthy. "We appear to be entering an era of prosperity which is gradually reaching into every part of the nation," Coolidge said.

◄ Coolidge giving a speech in 1925

Coolidge was only partly correct. During the 1920s, the United States did experience a boom, which is a period of wealth and prosperity. This time of peace and plenty became known as the Roaring Twenties. As president, Coolidge slashed taxes and lowered the nation's debt. Most Americans paid no taxes at all—the tax burden fell entirely upon the wealthy. However, trouble was beginning to brew. Thousands of Americans were without jobs or money. As Coolidge's term wore on, the gap between rich and poor continued to widen.

Part of the problem was Coolidge's belief in a laissez-faire economic policy. This meant that he was against laws that limited what big businesses could do. Coolidge's policies contributed to the serious economic problems that arose in the late 1920s, after he left office. During President Herbert Hoover's term, which followed Coolidge's, the nation was plunged into the **Great Depression**—its worst economic crisis ever.

As president, Coolidge surrounded himself with intelligent advisers. Secretary of the Treasury Andrew Mellon was a wealthy businessman. Secretary of Commerce Herbert Hoover would go on to become the thirty-first U.S. president. Secretary of State Frank B. Kellogg would later win the Nobel Peace Prize. Coolidge usually supported his advisers' actions and did little to interfere with them.

▼ *President Coolidge standing with Secretary of the Treasury Andrew Mellon (middle) and Secretary of Commerce Herbert Hoover*

Despite his habit of allowing events to run their course, Coolidge sometimes opposed Congress and even his own party when he believed they were wrong. For example, Congress passed a bill, or proposed law, called the Veterans Bonus Act in 1924. This bill awarded insurance policies to Americans who had served during World War I. Coolidge did not believe that any American should receive a handout, so he vetoed, or rejected, the bill. Congress, however, overturned the president's veto, and the bill became law.

Supporters of the ▾ Veterans Bonus Act stand in front of the White House.

In 1927, Coolidge disagreed once again with Congress when he vetoed the Farm Relief Bill. This bill was intended to help struggling farmers in the Midwest by having the federal government buy extra crops and sell them in Europe. Some historians believe that this bill might have prevented the Great Depression that hit the nation after Coolidge left office. However, the bill went against Coolidge's principle of staying out of private businesses. He believed that it favored certain groups of farmers over others. Coolidge also thought it encouraged farmers to produce too much of a single

▼ *Louisiana farmers planting sugarcane at about the same time Coolidge and Congress were disagreeing about the Farm Relief Bill*

crop, which he believed was at the root of the farmers' problem. When Congress passed a similar bill in 1928, Coolidge vetoed it as well.

While Coolidge kept a close eye on the U.S. economy, he was far less interested in foreign affairs. He believed that the United States should not allow itself to be drawn into quarrels between other countries. Still, Coolidge was very interested in trying to create world peace. In 1928, he supported the Kellogg-Briand **Treaty,** which had been developed by Secretary of State Kellogg

In support of the Kellogg-Briand Treaty were (from left, seated) Vice President Charles Dawes, President Calvin Coolidge, Secretary of State Frank Kellogg, and Secretary of the Treasury Andrew Mellon.

and Aristide Briand, a French official. The treaty, signed by sixty-two nations, attempted to outlaw war. Unfortunately, the document had little impact. Only a decade later, World War II (1939–1945) began in Europe.

In most matters relating to foreign countries, Coolidge allowed Kellogg to handle things. Coolidge agreed with Kellogg's decision to send U.S. troops to the Dominican Republic, Haiti, and Nicaragua to keep the peace and protect U.S. business interests.

▾ *U.S. soldiers unloading weapons in Nicaragua in 1927*

Coolidge refused to give France and Great Britain a break on the huge war debt they owed the United States. Again, Coolidge believed he was protecting U.S. interests. Although many people made fun of the president's stinginess, Coolidge refused to budge.

The Final Years

★ ★ ★

The cover of the New York Times reporting Coolidge's decision not to run for a second full term in 1928

As Coolidge's term neared an end, the nation waited to learn whether he would seek a second full term. Most people—including members of his own party—expected Coolidge to run for reelection. In August 1927, the president put an end to the guessing when he made the announcement that he would not run again. The news surprised everyone, even Grace Coolidge. She wrote later that she did not know her husband had decided to retire. Today, historians believe that grief over his son or his own ill health may have played a part in his choice.

As Coolidge looked back on his nearly six years in office, he was satisfied with the job he had done. At his last press conference as president, he said, "Perhaps one of the most important accomplishments of my administration has been minding my own business."

▾ *Calvin and Grace Coolidge (left) stand with Lou and Herbert Hoover, who will succeed them in the White House in 1929*

After leaving Washington, Coolidge kept busy. *The Autobiography of Calvin Coolidge* was published in 1929. In 1930, he wrote a daily newspaper column, "Calvin Coolidge Says," which was carried by many newspapers. He later wrote magazine articles.

The Coolidges returned to their half of the two-family home in Northampton. In his autobiography he explained, "I came from the people, [and] I wished to be one of them again." He quickly grew weary, however, of the parade of visitors who arrived on his front porch to pay their respects. Some even peeked in the

1923: Becomes 30th president of the United States after the death of President Harding. Coolidge is elected to a full term in office a year later.

1872: Born in Plymouth Notch, Vermont

As governor of Massachusetts, Coolidge's firm action in ending the Boston police strike of 1919 gains him the attention of the Republican Party.

windows to catch a glimpse of the former president and first lady. Before long, the Coolidges moved to an estate called the Beeches above the Connecticut River in Northampton.

▼ *Grace Coolidge watched as her husband cut his birthday cake at the Beeches in 1931. He turned fifty-nine on July 4.*

Coolidge was greatly upset by the economic depression that gripped the nation shortly after Herbert Hoover took office. As the years wore on, Coolidge felt more and more out of place in the world of politics. "I feel I no longer fit in with these times," he said during an interview. "We are in a new era to which I do not belong, and it would not be possible for me to adjust myself to it."

Calvin Coolidge died of a heart attack on January 5, 1933. He was only sixty years old. Coolidge was laid to rest in Plymouth Notch, Vermont, the small town that had shaped his character and remained in his heart throughout his life.

Calvin Coolidge's ◂ *grave in Plymouth Notch, Vermont*

CALVIN COOLIDGE

JULY 4, 1872

JANUARY 5, 1933

GLOSSARY

★ ★ ★

bribery—paying someone illegally to influence their opinions or actions

campaign—an organized effort to win an election

candidate—someone running for office in an election

Constitution—the document stating the basic laws of the United States

corruption—willingness to do things that are wrong or illegal

Great Depression—an era of severe unemployment and poverty in the United States that began with the October 1929 stock market crash; it lasted throughout the 1930s and was relieved by America's entry into World War II

laissez-faire—the belief that the government should not get involved in the economy

legislatures—the parts of government that make or change laws

militia—an army of part-time soldiers

press conferences—gatherings at which public figures answer questions from reporters

prosperity—economic well-being

strike—when workers refuse to work, hoping to force their company to agree to their demands

thrifty—not wasteful with money

treaty—an agreement between two governments

union—an organization of workers

CALVIN COOLIDGE'S LIFE AT A GLANCE

★ ★ ★

PERSONAL

Nickname:	Silent Cal
Born:	July 4, 1872
Birthplace:	Plymouth Notch, Vermont
Father's name:	John Calvin Coolidge
Mother's name:	Victoria Josephine Moor Coolidge
Education:	Graduated from Amherst College in 1895
Wife's Name:	Grace Anna Goodhue Coolidge (1879–1957)
Married:	October 4, 1905
Children:	John Coolidge (1906–2000); Calvin Coolidge (1908–1924)
Died:	January 5, 1933, in Northampton, Massachusetts
Buried:	Plymouth Notch, Vermont

PUBLIC

Occupation before presidency:	Lawyer, politician
Occupation after presidency:	Writer
Military service:	None
Other government positions:	Member of the Northampton City Council; member of the Massachusetts House of Representatives; mayor of Northampton; member of the Massachusetts Senate; lieutenant governor of Massachusetts; governor of Massachusetts; vice president
Political party:	Republican
Vice president:	Charles G. Dawes (1925–1929)
Dates in office:	August 3, 1923–March 3, 1929
Presidential opponents:	John W. Davis (Democrat) and Robert M. La Follette (Progressive), 1924
Number of votes (Electoral College):	15,718,211 of 28,934,783 (382 of 531), 1924
Writings:	*The Autobiography of Calvin Coolidge* (1929)

Calvin Coolidge's Cabinet

Secretary of state:
Charles Evans Hughes (1923–1925)
Frank B. Kellogg (1925–1929)

Secretary of the treasury:
Andrew W. Mellon (1923–1929)

Secretary of war:
John W. Weeks (1923–1925)
Dwight F. Davis (1925–1929)

Attorney general:
Harry M. Daugherty (1923–1924)
Harlan F. Stone (1924–1925)
John G. Sargent (1925–1929)

Postmaster general:
Harry S. New (1923–1929)

Secretary of the navy:
Edwin Denby (1923–1924)
Curtis D. Wilbur (1924–1929)

Secretary of the interior:
Hubert Work (1923–1928)
Roy O. West (1929)

Secretary of agriculture:
Henry C. Wallace (1923–1924)
Howard M. Gore (1924–1925)
William M. Jardine (1925–1929)

Secretary of commerce:
Herbert C. Hoover (1923–1928)
William F. Whiting (1928–1929)

Secretary of labor:
James J. Davis (1923–1929)

CALVIN COOLIDGE'S LIFE AND TIMES

★ ★ ★

COOLIDGE'S LIFE		WORLD EVENTS

COOLIDGE'S LIFE

July 4, Coolidge is born in Plymouth Notch, Vermont — 1872

Starts school in one room schoolhouse — 1877

1880

WORLD EVENTS

1876 — Alexander Graham Bell uses the first telephone to speak to his assistant, Thomas Watson

1877 — German inventor Nikolaus A. Otto works on what will become the internal combustion engine for automobiles

1882 — Thomas Edison builds a power station

1884 — Mark Twain publishes *The Adventures of Huckleberry Finn*

COOLIDGE'S LIFE

Coolidge's mother, 1885
Victoria Moor
Coolidge, dies

Graduates from Black 1890
River Academy

Graduates from 1895
Amherst College
(above)

Passes the law exams 1897
to become a lawyer

Elected to the 1898
Northampton,
Massachusetts,
city council

WORLD EVENTS

1886 Grover Cleveland
dedicates the Statue of
Liberty in New York

1891 The Roman Catholic
Church publishes the
encyclical *Rerum
Novarum,* which
supports the rights
of labor

1893 Women gain voting
privileges in New
Zealand, the first
country to take such
a step

1896 The Olympic Games
are held for the first
time in recent history in
Athens, Greece (below)

1890

COOLIDGE'S LIFE

Marries Grace Anna 1905
Goodhue (above)

Elected to the 1906
Massachusetts House
of Representatives

Becomes mayor of 1910
Northampton,
Massachusetts

Elected to 1911
Massachusetts Senate

WORLD EVENTS

1899   Isadora Duncan, one
of the founders of
modern dance, makes
her debut in Chicago

1903   Brothers Orville and
Wilbur Wright
(below) successfully
fly a powered airplane

1909   The National
Association for the
Advancement of
Colored People
(NAACP) is founded

1913   Henry Ford begins to
use standard assembly
lines to produce
automobiles (above)

1900

1910

COOLIDGE'S LIFE

Becomes president   1914
of the state senate

Elected lieutenant   1915
governor of
Massachusetts

Elected governor of   1918
Massachusetts

Ends a strike by the   1919
Boston police

Elected vice president of   1920
the United States with
Warren G. Harding
(below, left)

WORLD EVENTS

1914   Archduke Francis
Ferdinand is assassinated,
launching World War I
(1914–1918)

1916   German-born physicist
Albert Einstein (below)
publishes his general
theory of relativity

1919   World War I peace
conference begins at
Versailles, France

1920   American women get
the right to vote

1922   James Joyce
publishes *Ulysses*

The tomb of
Tutankhamen
is discovered by
British archaeologist
Howard Carter

1920

COOLIDGE'S LIFE

WORLD EVENTS

August 3, is sworn
in as president
after Warren G.
Harding dies   **1923**

The Teapot Dome
Scandal and
other scandals
from Harding's
administration
become public

Son Calvin dies from   **1924**
blood poisoning

1923   French actress Sarah
Bernhardt (above) dies

Presidential Election Results:	*Popular Votes*	*Electoral Votes*
1924 *Calvin Coolidge*	*15,718,211*	*382*
John W. Davis	*8,385,283*	*136*
Robert M. La Follette	*4,831,289*	*13*

1926   A.A. Milne (above)
publishes *Winnie
the Pooh*

Claude Monet and
Mary Cassat, well-
known impressionist
painters, die

COOLIDGE'S LIFE			WORLD EVENTS
Vetoes the Farm Relief Bill, which was intended to help Midwestern farmers	1927		
August, announces he will not seek another term			
Supports the Kellogg-Briand Treaty, which outlaws war	1928	1928	Penicillin, the first antibiotic, is discovered by Scottish scientist Alexander Fleming
Publishes *The Autobiography of Calvin Coolidge*	1929	1929	The United States stock exchange collapses and severe economic depression sets in
Dedicates the Coolidge Dam near Globe, Arizona	1930	**1930** 1930	Designs for the first jet engine are submitted to the Patent Office in Britain

January 5, dies in Northampton, Massachusetts, of a heart attack	1933	1933	Nazi leader Adolf Hitler (above) is named chancellor of Germany

UNDERSTANDING CALVIN COOLIDGE AND HIS PRESIDENCY

★ ★ ★

IN THE LIBRARY

Allen, Michael Geoffrey. *Calvin Coolidge.*
Berkeley Heights, N.J.: Enslow, 2002.

Joseph, Paul. *Calvin Coolidge.* Edina, Minn.: Abdo & Daughters, 2000.

Maupin, Melissa. *Calvin Coolidge: Our Thirtieth President.*
Chanhassen, Minn.: The Child's World, 2001.

ON THE WEB

Calvin Coolidge: 30th President of the United States
http://www.calvin-coolidge.org
For photos, cartoons, speeches, and biographical information

Internet Public Library—Calvin Coolidge
http://www.ipl.org/div/potus/ccoolidge.html
For information about Coolidge's presidency
and many links to other resources

The American President—Calvin Coolidge
http://www.americanpresident.org/KoTrain/Courses/CC/CC_In_Brief.htm
To read in-depth information about Calvin Coolidge

COOLIDGE HISTORIC SITES
ACROSS THE COUNTRY

President Calvin Coolidge State Historic Site
Plymouth Notch Historic District
P. O. Box 247
Plymouth, VT 05056
802/672-3773
To visit Coolidge's birthplace, boyhood home, and grave

Calvin Coolidge Presidential Library and Museum
Forbes Library
West Street
Northampton, MA 01060
413/587-1014
To learn more about the life and work of Coolidge

THE U.S. PRESIDENTS
(Years in Office)

★ ★ ★

1. **George Washington**
   (March 4, 1789–March 3, 1797)
2. **John Adams**
   (March 4, 1797–March 3, 1801)
3. **Thomas Jefferson**
   (March 4, 1801–March 3, 1809)
4. **James Madison**
   (March 4, 1809–March 3, 1817)
5. **James Monroe**
   (March 4, 1817–March 3, 1825)
6. **John Quincy Adams**
   (March 4, 1825–March 3, 1829)
7. **Andrew Jackson**
   (March 4, 1829–March 3, 1837)
8. **Martin Van Buren**
   (March 4, 1837–March 3, 1841)
9. **William Henry Harrison**
   (March 6, 1841–April 4, 1841)
10. **John Tyler**
    (April 6, 1841–March 3, 1845)
11. **James K. Polk**
    (March 4, 1845–March 3, 1849)
12. **Zachary Taylor**
    (March 5, 1849–July 9, 1850)
13. **Millard Fillmore**
    (July 10, 1850–March 3, 1853)
14. **Franklin Pierce**
    (March 4, 1853–March 3, 1857)
15. **James Buchanan**
    (March 4, 1857–March 3, 1861)
16. **Abraham Lincoln**
    (March 4, 1861–April 15, 1865)
17. **Andrew Johnson**
    (April 15, 1865–March 3, 1869)

18. **Ulysses S. Grant**
    (March 4, 1869–March 3, 1877)
19. **Rutherford B. Hayes**
    (March 4, 1877–March 3, 1881)
20. **James Garfield**
    (March 4, 1881–Sept 19, 1881)
21. **Chester Arthur**
    (Sept 20, 1881–March 3, 1885)
22. **Grover Cleveland**
    (March 4, 1885–March 3, 1889)
23. **Benjamin Harrison**
    (March 4, 1889–March 3, 1893)
24. **Grover Cleveland**
    (March 4, 1893–March 3, 1897)
25. **William McKinley**
    (March 4, 1897–
    September 14, 1901)
26. **Theodore Roosevelt**
    (September 14, 1901–
    March 3, 1909)
27. **William Howard Taft**
    (March 4, 1909–March 3, 1913)
28. **Woodrow Wilson**
    (March 4, 1913–March 3, 1921)
29. **Warren G. Harding**
    (March 4, 1921–August 2, 1923)
30. Calvin Coolidge
    (August 3, 1923–March 3, 1929)
31. **Herbert Hoover**
    (March 4, 1929–March 3, 1933)
32. **Franklin D. Roosevelt**
    (March 4, 1933–April 12, 1945)

33. **Harry S. Truman**
    (April 12, 1945–
    January 20, 1953)
34. **Dwight D. Eisenhower**
    (January 20, 1953–
    January 20, 1961)
35. **John F. Kennedy**
    (January 20, 1961–
    November 22, 1963)
36. **Lyndon B. Johnson**
    (November 22, 1963–
    January 20, 1969)
37. **Richard M. Nixon**
    (January 20, 1969–
    August 9, 1974)
38. **Gerald R. Ford**
    (August 9, 1974–
    January 20, 1977)
39. **James Earl Carter**
    (January 20, 1977–
    January 20, 1981)
40. **Ronald Reagan**
    (January 20, 1981–
    January 20, 1989)
41. **George H. W. Bush**
    (January 20, 1989–
    January 20, 1993)
42. **William Jefferson Clinton**
    (January 20, 1993–
    January 20, 2001)
43. **George W. Bush**
    (January 20, 2001–)

INDEX

★   ★   ★

ABOUT THE AUTHOR

Robin S. Doak has been writing for children for more than fourteen years. A former editor of *Weekly Reader* and *U*S*Kids* magazine, Ms. Doak has authored fun and educational materials for kids of all ages. Some of her work includes biographies of explorers such as Henry Hudson and John Smith, as well as other titles in this series. Ms. Doak is a past winner of an Educational Press Association of America Distinguished Achievement Award. She lives with her husband and three children in central Connecticut.